The Garden Of Her Scars

Scars

From Roots To Rise

Dhivyah Raju

BookLeaf
Publishing

India | USA | UK

Dedication

For every woman who has ever carried her pain in silence -
This is for you.

For the hearts that broke quietly,
and the souls that learned to smile through their scars.
For the ones who loved deeply, lost deeply,
and still found the strength to bloom again.

For the mothers, daughters, and dreamers
who gave too much and were left with too little,
yet never stopped believing in light.

For those who prayed when words failed,
who healed themselves when help never came,
and who chose kindness even when the world was
unkind.

For you -
the woman who became her own miracle,
who turned her wounds into wisdom,
and her sorrow into song.

May these pages remind you

that your scars are not the end of your story -
they are the roots of your garden.
You are proof that grace never leaves,
and that even in silence,
the soul continues to bloom.

"She didn't just survive -
She became beautiful in the places she was broken."

Preface

Author's Note

This book is not written to hurt, insult, or blame anyone.
It is written to honour every woman who has walked
through darkness
and found even the smallest light of her own strength.

Garden of Her Scars is a reflection -
not of anger, but of awakening.
It speaks for those who suffered in silence,
who were broken but did not stay broken,
who chose to rise from sorrow instead of surrendering to
it.

Each poem is a reminder that no matter what you've
faced,
you still carry the power to heal, to forgive, and to bloom
again.
Your scars are not your shame - they are your story,
and your story is sacred.

*"This is not a tale of blame -
it is a tribute to survival."*

There are some stories that do not grow from joy,
but from the soil of sorrow - watered by tears, nourished
by hope.
Garden Of Her Scars is one such story.

It is a collection of reflections and poems that speak of a
woman's quiet strength -
her pain, her faith, her endurance, and her gentle
transformation.
Every scar she carries is not a mark of shame,
but proof of her survival - a bloom that grew where she
once bled.

This book is not about suffering; it is about rebirth.
It is about how pain can be both teacher and seed,
how loss can carve space for light,
and how grace can find us even when we no longer
believe in it.

Each poem here is a step -
through heart break, through loneliness, through
forgiveness,
toward the peace that waits beyond all fear.
It is written for every woman who has been
misunderstood,
every soul who has been silenced,

and every heart that has learned to smile through pain.

The Garden of Her Scars is not a place of sorrow -
it is sacred ground.
it is where she remembers who she is,
where she learns that beauty does not come from being
unbroken,
but from blooming anyway.

May these words remind you of your own quiet power.
May they heal what still hurts,
and help you see that even your scars are divine -

each one petal, each one story,
each one proof that you survived.

"Her scars were never flaws -
they were flowers, learning to live in the light."

Acknowledgements

For The Garden of Her Scars

This book was not born in silence; it grew from the voices, hands, and hearts that held me when I could no longer hold myself.

To the woman who came before me - mothers, grandmothers, and the quiet ones whose pain was never spoken - this story is your lessons, your sacrifices, and your echoes in everything I write.

To the readers - the ones who have walked through their own garden of Scars- thank you for opening these pages with open hearts.

If they bring even a moment of comfort,
if they remind you of your own divine light,
then this garden has bloomed as it was meant to.

And finally, to the life itself -
for teaching me that even in loss, there is learning.
and even in pain, there is purpose.

"These scars are not endings -

they are the beginnings that chose to grow."

1. Her First Bloom

She came with the whisper of morning light,
A tender soul, so pure, so bright.
The world stood still - the angels sighed,
A flower opened, the stars replied.

Wrapped in warmth, in arms so deep,
She breathed her first, then fell asleep.
The lullaby of life began,
A rhythm soft.

Her eyes were oceans, calm and wide,
Where dreams and wonder both reside.
Each smile she wore, the heavens knew,
The earth felt soft, the skies turned blue.

Tiny fingers, curled with grace,
Reached for love, for time, for space.
The moon leaned close to kiss her cheek,
As silence spoke what words can't speak.

She learned to crawl, to stand, to fall,
To chase her echoes down the hall.
Her laughter floated through the air,
So full of joy, so light, so rare.

The flowers bowed where she would play,
Her feet like whispers on their way.
She found in dust a golden gleam,
She found in shadows one more dream.

The stories told beside her bed,
Would dance like stars inside her head.
She dreamed of wings, of skies so high,
Of songs that taught her how to fly.

The world was vast - she was so small,
Yet hope and wonder crowned it all.
A child of peace, of love, of bloom,
She filled each heart, she lit each room.

Before the storm, before the fight,
Before she learned of wrong and right -
She lived in colours soft and mild,
The Sacred season of a child.

And though the years will shape her name,
And time will never leave her same -

The world will always find perfume,
In memories of Her First Bloom.

Quote for every soul:

*"She was not born to be perfect -
she was born to be real,
to grow, to feel, to bloom."*

2. Her Growing Skies

The child has grown - her laughter stays,
But now it sings in wiser ways.
Her eyes, once wide with simple glee,
Now search for who she wants to be.

The world expands - so bright, so vast,
Each moment echoes from her past.
She learned that hearts can bloom and break,
That love is gentle, yet can ache.

She stands between the dusk and dawn,
Half still a child, half nearly grown.
Her dreams grow tall, her fears grow small,
She learns the weight, the worth of all.

The mirror shows a changing face,
Soft lines of thought, of poise, of grace.
A spark within begins to shine -
The voice that whispers, "I am mine."

She writes her hopes on paper wings,
And trusts the wind with secret things.
Her laughter now - both strong and sweet,
A rhythm life will not defeat.

The friends she finds, the truth she learns,
The light within her softly burns.
She questions stars, she talks to rain,
She dances through both joy and pain.

The sky above - her growing stage,
Each year, a turn, Each tear, a page.
She's not the budget she used to be,
But not yet all the world will see.

Her hands still hold the scent of play,
Yet reach for dreams far, far away.
Her heart begins to understand,
The pulse of time, the shift of sand.

And though confusion clouds her sight,
She walks with courage towards the light.
For deep inside, she starts to know,
The winds of womanhood will blow.

She learns that strength is born from care,
That beauty's truth is found in dare.

And every doubt, and every sigh,
Becomes a star in her own sky.

So let her rise, through joy, through cries -
A bloom now meeting open skies.
For she, once soft as morning dew,
Now learns the world - and all that's true.

Her journey hums, her spirit flies -
Forever growing...Her Growing Skies.

Quote for Her Growing Skies

*"The world was bigger than her fears,
and her dreams started to rise
like morning clouds unafraid of light."*

3. Her Hidden Sun

She walks beneath a walking sky,
A hush of hope where dreams still lie.
The child she was has flown from sight,
But left her heart forever bright.

No crown she wears, no loud acclaim,
Yet life itself now speaks her name.
Her voice is calm, her gaze is clear -
The world grows softer when she's near.

She learns that strength is not to shout,
But standing tall when lights go out.
In quiet grace, she meets the day,
And turns her pain to gentle clay.

Her hands have known both loss and care,
Her heart still open, stripped, yet fair.
She builds from ashes, love from Scars,
And finds her peace among the stars.

The fire she holds, she hides from sight,
It glows within, a secret light.
She warms the world with steady glow,
While few will see the depths below.

Her laughter now is calm and wide,
A healing wave, a turning tide.
She give, she breaks, she mends again,
She walks through storms as through soft rain.

The mirror shows both grace and ache,
The years she's lived, the roads they make.
Each wrinkle, line, and fading hue,
A map of all that she's come through.

She loves with depth the sky can't hold,
A quiet tale the stars resold.
Her touch can melt the touch of fear,
Her silence speaks - the strong draw near.

She needs no praise, no fleeting flame,
Her worth outshines the weight of fame.
For deep within, the light is spun -
A timeless glow, Her Hidden Sun.

Quote for every heart:

"She poured all her light into love, forgetting that the glow had always been her own."

4. Her Veiled Sacrifice

She left her wings beside the door,
and stepped inside a smaller sky.
The world had called it happiness,
and so she learned to try.

She stitched her laughter into walls,
her hopes into the evening tea.
The dreams once written in her hands
were folded, quietly.

She gave the voices to gentler tones,
her hours to rooms that never slept.
Each smile She wore was soft disguise,
for promises She kept.

The mirror knew what eyes forgot -
the girl who dreamed of something wide.
Yet peace was born from patient breath,
and tears she chose to hide.

She build her world on humble ground,
each heartbeat held by faith alone.
And though she vanished piece by piece,
her grace had never flown.

A whisper lived beneath her pain -
a secret flame, a steady hue:
Love asks for sharing, not for loss;
the truest vow begins in you.

Quote for Her Veiled Sacrifice:

"In loving, she forgot herself -
and in losing herself,
she learned what love is not."

5. Her Golden Cradle

The years grew soft beneath her hands,
as laughter echoed through the air.
Two little hearts became her world,
two tiny suns to light her care.

She rocked the nights that would not end,
sang lullabies through unseen tears.
Each sleepless hour became her prayer,
each morning - proof she conquered fears.

The house was small, but full of song,
the meals were simple, full of grace.
She taught them love by giving all,
and wore devotion on her face.

Her arms were tired, her back was sore,
Yet joy still bloomed in every chore.
The world might never see her crown,
but angels knew what she knelt down for.

Through fevered cries and quiet dreams,
through mess and noise and gentle schemes
She builds a home of patient peace,
and found her heaven there, in these.

No riches came, no praises loud,
but still she stood serene, unbowed.
For love like hers will never fade -
It's born, it breaks, it still forgives.

And when they slept, her eyes would close,
to whisper soft what mothers, know:
"I am enough, though none may see
their breath, their smiles -
they worship me."

Quote for Her Golden Cradle:

*"In her arms, the world found peace -
even when she had none left for herself."*

6. Her Hidden Abundance

The cupboards whispered hollow hymns,
the lamp burned low, the nights were long.
Yet in her hands, the world felt warm -
her heart still sang a steadfast song.

No jewels adorned her gentle grace,
no praise, no gold, no grand display.
But kindness bloomed in every chore,
and peace walked softly where she'd stay.

She wove her worries into prayer,
turned emptiness to quiet art.
The things she had could never match
the treasures blooming in her heart.

A torn old sari, neatly pressed,
became her robe of quiet pride.
Her calm was wealth, her smile her crown,
her faith the gold she kept inside.

She learned that hunger sharpens soul,
that giving sweetens what remains.
That joy can rise from simple bread,
and love can live through loss and strains.

No one could see what she possessed -
they saw her lack, but not her light.
For those who count in coins and things
can't measure hearts that glow at night.

Her wealth was not of purse or land,
but courage held in steady hands.
A richness pure, beyond expense -
the grace of quiet confidence.

Quote for next generation:

*"True abundance lives unseen -
not in your purse, but in your peace."*

7. Her Silent Season

The house grew quiet, day by day,
her laughter softly slipped away.
The air was filled with folded sighs,
and light grew faint with weary eyes

The mornings came with measured grace,
her tasks repeated, face by face.
No anger showed, no word was thrown -
she built her calm from pain alone.

Her voice became a distant sound,
a whisper lost, yet still profound.
The wall could hear what none could see -
her prayers disguised as memory.

She moved like peace, though peace was gone,
still faithful to what love had drawn.
Her silence spoke of something more,
a courage quiet to the core.

The world believed her spirit still,
but underneath was iron will.
Each glance, each nod, each soft refrain -
a vow that she would rise again.

For even in her muted place,
her heart held warmth, her soul held space.
And what seemed silence, cold and bare,
was strength in bloom - beyond despair.

This was her season, long and deep,
where lessons root, where angels weep.
Where stillness teaches how to see,
and pain refine identity.

Quote for every woman:

*"Silence is not surrender -
sometimes it's the soil where strength begins to grow."*

8. The Rule Of Silence

She learned the language few could name -
the quite life, the tempered flame.
A world that asked her not to speak,
but smile instead, and stay discreet.

Each word she held became too loud,
each thought too bright, each hope too proud.
So she began to fold her dreams,
and stitched her truth along the seams.

The air grew thick with *"yes and "must"*,
obedience became her trust.
she learned to read the room's command,
to speak through eyes, not open hand.

The years went by in muted hues,
her laughter caged, her courage bruised.
The world admired her steady grace -
not knowing what it had erased.

But silence, though it binds and bends,
can also teach where power ends.
And in that hush, she found her core -
the voice she'd lost began to soar.

It whispered softly through her pain,
"you can be whole, you can remain."
The quiet made her see within,
where strength was waiting to begin.

So though she spoke in careful tone,
inside her grew a world her own.
The rule of silence could not chain
the woman learning through her pain.

Quote for every soul:

*"When they silence your voice,
let your silence teach them how strength sounds."*

9. The Weight Of Unseen Tears

The nights grew long, the rooms grew still,
the walls absorbed her quiet will.
She smiled as the ache was small,
and held her world from sudden fall.

The pillow learned what eyes concealed,
the dreams she lost, the wounds unhealed.
Each tear she shed, a secret prayer,
each breath - a plea for lighter air.

She spoke to no one of her pain,
her sorrow hid in gentle rain.
By dawn, she wiped her trace clean,
and wore composure, calm, serene.

The neighbours saw her steady grace,
the perfect calm for upon her face.
They never guessed how hard she tried,
to keep the breaking locked inside.

But tears unspoken find their way,
through heart, through bone, through silent day.
And even still, she did not yield -
her love remained, her wounds concealed.

She cooked, she cared, she worked, she prayed,
through every storm her peace was made.
For though the world could not appear,
her strength was born from every tear.

Each sorrow pressed became her guide,
each ache refined the flame inside.
She learned that pain could cleanse, not kill,
and silence too can show god's will.

Quote for every heart:

*"You never truly see a woman's strength
until you've watched her smile with eyes
that just cried."*

10. Her Endless Bloom

She carried hope in quiet hands,
like petal saved from storms and sand.
Though seasons passed and colours waned,
her faith in love still softly rained.

She waited not for praise or sign,
but trusted time, the grand design.
Each wound she bore became her seed,
each tear, a drop her roots would need.

Her laughter dimmed, her world was small,
yet kindness held her through it all.
She found her peace in daily grace,
a gentle light upon her face.

The world had changed, her dreams had too,
but something bright still breathed anew.
A tenderness she could not name,
a strength that never asked for fame.

For even when her heart was tired,
her spirit bloomed - still, never mired.
No voice could wilt what lived inside,
no loss could take what faith supplied.

She learned that love is not return,
but giving more than one could earn.
That hope, once sown in honest ground,
will always find its way around.

And though her story's lined with pain,
the fragrance of her soul remains.
For hearts like hers - though tried, though scarred -
bloom endless, bright, and unbegrudged.

Quote for every woman:

*"The world may take your petals,
but it cannot touch your roots."*

11. The Spark Beneath the Ash

Beneath the weight of passing years,
beneath the salt of buried tears,
a whisper stirred - too faint to see,
a spark of what she used to be.

It flickered first in restless dreams,
in golden light through broken seams.
In tasks once dull, she felt a call -
a quiet pulse beneath it all.

She could not name the change she felt,
nor trace the ground where courage knelt.
But deep within, the ashes moved -
and from her heart, her soul approved.

A thought took root: *"I still remain"*,
A tiny truth, born out of pain.
It glowed against the dark and cold,
a promise whispered, small and bold.

Her voice returned in fragile tones,
her laughter echoed through the stones.
She smiled, unsure, but dared to start -
to feed the fire inside her heart.

No grand revolt, no sudden cry -
just steady light that reached the sky.
For change is slow, and healing too,
but sparks, once freed, know what to do.

The world still thought she wore her chains,
but freedom pulsed within her veins.
And in her eyes, the dawn was seen -
the glow of what she might have been.

Quote for every heart:

*"No matter how long the night,
the ember of who you are
never forgets how to burn."*

12. Her Unheard Wings

In secret hours, when nights were kind,
she stitched her thoughts and healed her mind.
The world still slept, the stars still burned -
and in the hush, her spirit turned.

She gathered courage, thread by thread,
from words once said and tears once shed.
Each failure she had buried deep
became the ground her dreams would keep.

No trumpet called, no voices praised,
no spotlight glowed, no banner raised.
But quietly, beneath the noise,
she built her strength, reclaimed her poise.

She learned again to trust her hands,
to make, to write, to understand -
that even pain can shape the soul,
and wounds can carve what makes us whole.

Her wings were small, her steps unsure,
but each attempt made faith endure.
For flight begins not in the air,
but deep within - with self-repair.

No one could see her gentle fight,
her lessons learned in borrowed light.
Yet every dawn her will had grown,
and grace began to call her home.

She rose in silence, calm, unseen,
the world unaware of what she'd been.
Her wings were unheard - soft, not proud -
but soon they'd lift her past the cloud.

Quote for every woman:

"Grow quietly; the world will notice when you fly."

13. Her Rising Stone

She built her days from patient clay,
her nights from whispers, soft and true.
No one applauded what she made,
but every dawn, her courage grew.

The world still saw the same old face,
the gentle hands, the tempered grace.
They never guessed the storms she'd braved,
nor how her faith had carved her brave.

She worked in silence, heart by heart,
and turned her sorrow into art.
No task too small, no dream too late -
her purpose rose, deliberate.

The stones she carried - doubt, regret -
became the walls her strength would set.
Each burden laid became a base,
each scar - a mark of sacred grace.

She learned that worth was self-defined,
that peace was earned, not merely kind.
She did not beg the world to see -
she built her proof in legacy.

For when the world had turned away,
she learned to bless herself and stay.
And from the weight that once confined,
She raised a life - both firm and kind.

Her rising stone - her patient art -
a monument to her own heart.

Quote for every woman who builds herself back:

*"You are the architect of your becoming -
even ruins can rise into temple."*

14. Her Fractured Flame

Her light had grown, a steady gleam,
a calm within her waking dream.
But shadows moved through friendly doors,
and peace was shaken to its core.

A whisper dressed in gentle guise,
a comfort with a hidden prize.
It crept between her trust and will,
and left her trembling - quiet, still.

The warmth she'd kindled dimmed once more,
the glow she'd tended touched the floor.
Yet even in that flickering space,
her heart refused to lose its grace.

She did not shout, she did not fight,
she simply held her flame in sight.
Though fear had tried to draw her in,
her faith stayed firm beneath the din.

For kindness doesn't end with pain,
and mercy blooms where loss has lain.
She let the echo fade away,
and faced her dusk without dismay.

Her love had been misunderstood,
her loyalty repaid with lies.
But truth is quiet, never cruel,
and time will sift through all disguise.

She rose again - her fire intact,
though smaller now, and more exact.
She learned that not all warmth is true,
that some bright lights can burn you blue.

Yet still she glowed, though faint and slow,
for broken flames still learn to grow.
Her strength became her candle's hue -
a faith refined, and pure, and new.

Quote for every soul tested by betrayal:

*"Some losses come to teach you
which light is truly yours."*

15. Her Shattered Moon

The moon she held began to fade,
its silver light turned cold and grey.
The vows she whispered once with faith
were scattered now, in soft decay.

No storm announced the breaking dawn,
no shout, no tear, no loud goodbye.
just silence thick as winter's breath,
just truth too heavy not to cry.

The walls she built to shelter love
now echoed empty, hollow tones.
Her hands still searched fir what was gone,
but found instead her heart - alone.

The air was filled with what was lost,
with memories stitched to gentle lies.
Yet even in her quiet grief,
a fire was born behind her eyes.

She walked through rooms still holding ghosts,
their laughter faint, their shadows near.
And in her chest, the ache would pulse,
both wound and warning, prayer and fear.

But pain can carve what words can't reach,
and sorrow teaches what love hides.
In losing all she thought was hers,
she met the truth she'd been denied.

The moon was shattered - yes, it's true -
but broken things can still bring light.
Its pieces gleamed along her path,
to guide her through the longest night.

Quote for every woman who's been left:

*"Some endings are not punishment -
they are protection, disguised as pain."*

16. Her Depth Of Night

The night was tide, without a shore,
a sea of loss, forevermore.
The stars had dimmed, the wind stood still -
her heart, a field the frost would fill.

She walked through hours without name,
each breath a memory, each sigh a flame.
The silence pressed, the shadows stayed,
and hope grew faint, but never frayed.

Her tears fell slow, like holy rain,
each one a thread that eased the pain.
For sorrow, when it's faced alone,
can polish grief into a stone.

She clutched that stone - her only friend,
and prayed for wounds she could not mend.
No voices came, no rescue near,
just faith that whispered through the fear.

The dark became her teacher's hand,
the ache, a truth she'd understand:
that even night, when loved enough,
reveals a sky of stars above.

She did not beg the pain to part,
she let it wash, she let it start.
And when it passed, she saw, so clear -
her soul was lighter for each tear.

For deep below what eyes can see,
the heart learns strength in misery.
And there she found her truest might -
the grace to walk without the light.

Quote for every heart in darkness:

*"Do not curse the night that breaks you -
it is teaching you how to glow."*

17. Her Sacred Storm

The wind returned - fierce, untamed, real,
demanding all she'd learned to feel.
No longer calm, no longer small,
she faced her truth and risked the fall.

Her heart had cracked, her voice had fled,
but now the words she'd never said
rose like rain that had waited years -
a flood made pure by silent tears.

The thunder spoke the things she knew,
the lightning flashed her spirit through.
She stood within her pain, unbowed -
no longer meek, no longer cowed.

Each cry became a battle hymn,
each scar a mark of faith within.
The world had tried to hush her fire,
but storms don't end - they just inspire.

She broke the chains that held her name,
refused to shoulder borrowed blame.
And in the chaos, found release -
a wild surrender, fierce in peace.

The sky did not destroy her form,
she was the sky - she was the storm.
And when the thunder passed away,
she stood reborn, in light and clay.

For storms don't come to tear apart,
they come to cleanse a weary heart.
And in her wake of rain and flame,
she learned her power had no name.

Quote for every woman who survived her breaking:

"The storm you fear is the strength you are becoming."

18. Her Wild Garden

The storm was gone, the sky was bare,
the world still smelled of rain and prayer.
Her hands, once trembling, met the ground,
and felt new life beneath it found.

She planted dreams in broken clay,
and watched them grow in their own way.
No careful rows, no rules, no plan -
just faith and sunlight, breath and span.

The weeds of grief still brushed her knees,
but flowers bloomed among the leaves.
And every scar the soil could see
became the root of empathy.

She worked in silence, slow and sure,
her heart more open, clean, and pure.
Each dawn she met with steady grace,
and peace began to take its place.

No longer seeking praise or part,
she built her life from her own heart.
Her children's laughter filled the air,
their joy became her answered prayer.

She didn't chase what once was gone;
she bloomed where she had been undone.
Her wild garden, rich and deep,
was born of all she chose to keep.

It wasn't perfect, neat, or planned -
but beauty bowed to her command.
For only those who've walked through pain
can make the desert bloom again.

Quote for every woman rebuilding herself:

*"Every broken soil can bloom -
if you water it with faith."*

19. Her Silent Fire

Her fire no longer roared or burned,
it glowed - a warmth the years had earned.
No more the flame of restless youth,
but light refined by loss and truth.

She no longer begged the world to see,
for peace had made her dignity.
Her worth no longer wore a crown,
she ruled by standing - not bowing down.

The world still spoke, but she stayed still,
anchored deep in her quiet will.
The storms could come, the winds could sway,
but her faith no longer blew away.

Her hand had built, her soul had healed,
her heart now opened, unconcealed.
She loved again - not to be known,
but just to give, and call it home.

The noise outside could not ignite
the calm that lived within her light.
For silence, once a cage of pain,
was now her strength, her soft domain.

She walked through crowds with eyes serene,
no pride, no fear, no in - between.
For those who've burned and learned and healed,
carry the sun their scars revealed.

Her silent fire - her sacred peace,
the kind that ends, yet brings release.
Not loud, not sharp, but purely whole -
a steady flame, a shining soul.

Quote for every woman who's learned peace:

*"The strongest fire does not roar -
it glows quietly and never dies."*

20. Her Sacred Solitude

The noise was gone, the crowd grew thin,
the silence turned to friend within.
What once felt lonely, cold, and wide,
became the space where peace would hide.

No longer needing who had gone,
she lit her lamp and journeyed on.
The love she sought in hearts of clay
was found in breath, in dawn, in day.

She spoke to God in simple ways -
through washing cups, through work, through praise.
And though no voice replied aloud,
she felt his nearness in the cloud.

The world had left, but not unkind -
their absence cleared her seeking mind.
Each echo faded into rest;
her own soft pulse became her guest.

She learned that being whole alone
is where the soul becomes its own.
That solitude, once feared and vast,
is love that finally learned to last.

She smiled without a need to prove,
she moved in peace that would not move.
And those who saw her, calm and bright,
could feel her stillness in the light.

Her sacred solitude - her prayer,
her healing folded into air.
No longer half, no longer torn -
she bloomed again, complete, reborn.

Quote for every woman who's learned to stand alone:

"When you make peace with your solitude, you'll never feel alone again."

21. Her Eternal Grace

The road behind was lined with pain,
yet now it gleamed with gentle rain.
Each scar she bore had turned to gold,
each wound a truth her heart had told.

She left the past without goodbye,
no need to ask, no need to try.
For peace had whispered, kind and clear -
"You've done your part, you're free from here."

No bitterness remained to keep,
no rage to burn, no vow to weep.
Forgiveness came, not begged or forced,
but like a river finding course.

The hands once trembling now were sure,
the eyes once dim now calm, secure.
She walked in grace, unbound, untied -
a queen no crown could ever hide.

The world that broke her could not claim
the strength that rose beneath her name.
For all she lost, she gained instead
a soul reborn, a life widespread.

She did not need a grant return,
her heart no longer sought to earn.
Her worth was quiet, vast, complete -
a sacred rhythm, soft and sweet.

She prayed not for what used to be,
but thanked the pain that made her free.
For all that left had cleared the space
for peace to come and take its place.

And as she walked through dawn's new light,
her steps were steady, pure, and bright.
She smiled - not proud, not torn, not late -
just whole, and kind, and filled with faith.

Her story closed where it began,
with open heart and open hand.
And heaven knew, as earth now sees -
a woman born of broken peace.

Quote for every soul that

chooses peace:

"Let go with grace, not grief -
what leaves was never meant to stay.
Peace is not found - it is remembered."

22. Epilogue: "Her Becoming Light."

～～✕～～

She no longer walked - she flowed.
Every step a prayer, every breath a hymn.
The storms she'd faced now bowed to her calm,
the fire she'd tamed glowed within.

no crown adorned her silver hair,
no jewels, no need for show or glare.
Her silence spoke what words could not -
that peace once lost is never forgot.

The world that once had watched her fall
now whispered softly, she became all.
For from her pain, new gardens grew,
and others bloomed just passing through.

Her laughter now was calm, complete,
her kindness steady, soft, discreet.
She taught by living - not by speech,
her light reached hearts she'd never reach.

She'd found that love need not remain,
to leave its warmth, to end her pain.
She'd learned that endings are release,
and solitude is sacred peace.

No blame, no pride, no marks of war -
just quiet faith in who we are.
The one who lost, who knelt, who cried,
now lived unbound, clarified.

Her strength was no longer loud or raw,
it shimmered softly, pure with awe.
For those who watched her rise again,
she was proof: God lives in woman.

And when the evening met her eyes,
the sky reflected her replies.
For every star that lit the sea
was once a wound - now mastery.

She had become what time could not:
a soul fulfilled, a heart untaught.
Her story ended where light began -
not woman only - but human plan.

She smiled - and heaven took her side,

as moon and sun in her complied.
For she had bloomed beyond her pain,
and never would be dimmed again.

Final Reflection for every soul:

*"Do not rush to be loved -
become light instead.
The right hearts will find you
when you shine."*

23. Final Verdict

After all the storms, the silence, and the waiting -
she learned that life was never meant to be perfect,
only honest.

Every scar she carried had a reason,
every ending a quiet mercy.
What she once called loss was simply God's way of
giving her back to herself.

She no longer asked why me -
she whispered thank you.
For the pain that became her teacher,
for the love that showed her depth,
and for the solitude that revealed her soul.

Her journey was never about proving her worth -
it was about remembering it.
The world tried to define her by what she endured,
but she chose instead to be known by how she healed.

She stopped chasing closure from people and found it
instead in prayer,
in peace, in her own reflection.
No revenge. No bitterness.
Only release.

Her scars remained - not as reminders of hurt,
but as holy patterns of survival.
They were her flowers,
her proof that pain can transform into purpose when
touched by faith.

In the end, she didn't need the world to understand her -
only to feel her light.
Because she had become everything she once needed:
her own comfort, her own courage, her own grace.

And so, her final verdict was simple:
She forgave. She healed. She let go. She rose.

"I am not what happened to me -
I am what i chose to grow from it."

24. When You Close These Pages

Dear Soul,

When you close these pages,
I hope your heart feels little lighter -
not because the pain is gone,
but because you've learned to hold it more gently.

If these words have met you in a quiet moment,
I pray they remind you that your scars
were never signs of weakness,
but proof that you chose to survive.

Every poem you've read is a fragment of healing -
a whisper of grace, a trace of light.
They were written for the woman who has wept in
silence,
for the heart that still trembles,
for the soul that keeps rising, even when no one sees.

May you leave this book knowing that you are not alone.
may you see that pain is not the end - it is the beginning.
May you believe that every ending carries a seed of
something -
soft and holy waiting to grow.

When you close these pages,
remember - your scars have become your garden.
They are not what broke you.
they are what made you bloom.

Thank you for walking through her journey,
for feeling her silence, for breathing her strength.
If even one line touched your heart,
then this book has found its purpose.

Go gently, with grace.
Let faith be your sunlight.
Let love - even the lost kind - make you kind.
And when the world forgets your light,
remember: it's still burning within you.

"Her story ended not in pain,
but in peace -
a garden blooming quietly beneath her scars."

With love and light,
DHIVYAH RAJU.

www.ingramcontent.com/pod-product-compliance
Lightning Source LLC
Chambersburg PA
CBHW060353050426

42449CB00011B/2966